FROM ONE EXTREME TO THE OTHER

KERRY MITCHELL

A Birdy Black Book

Copyright © 2018 by **Kerry Mitchell**

All rights reserved. No part of this publication may be reproduced, distributed or transmitted in any form or by any means, without prior written permission.

Birdy Black Books
Melbourne

Publisher's Note: This is a work of fiction. Names, characters, places, and incidents are a product of the author's imagination. Locales and public names are sometimes used for atmospheric purposes. Any resemblance to actual people, living or dead, or to businesses, companies, events, institutions, or locales is completely coincidental.

Book Layout © 2017 BookDesignTemplates.com
Printed by Ingram Spark USA

From One Extreme to the Other/ Kerry Mitchell. -- 1st ed.
ISBN 978-0-6482301-0-6

These wonderful words
Are for the birds

These wings
These marvellous things

Were meant to fly
Said I

WHO

Who is this creature who lies so still
That you think she's not worth the trouble until

She opens her mouth and emotions pore out
But do you know what she's all about?

She is not rotten to the core
She is not a child anymore

She will raise her voice
She does have a choice

She will not believe your lies
She will shed her disguise

She is worth more than what you say
And she will escape from you one day

FEAR

I stretch but cannot reach
My life reflects an empty beach

My tide goes in, my tide goes out
Never reaching beyond my doubt

All I want in this sea of despair
Is to rise above water and breathe the fresh air

Why must the price I pay be so dear
When all that I want is to overcome fear

I DREAM

I dream of riding in a balloon
Reaching, aiming for the moon

If I don't make it tonight, tonight
I'll try again in the morning light

WHEN THINGS GO WRONG

I slam the door and
Damn!
Break a heel
My stocking slides across the floor
I rip a hole
Into it
The key to which the door is locked
Leaps gaily from my desperate clutch
Singing down the drain
I will not cry
I hope
Here comes the grotesque bus
I run
I trip
I fall
I curse
The bus laughs
On and on

HARSH WORDS

This hurt is not a shield
You're wrong if you think it's healed

Know that I can see what this brings
Our friendship destroyed by such petty things

THE DYING ROMANCE

Fondling, fumbling
Marlon Brando mumbling

Touching, scratching
Kisses that are catching

Coolness, no less
Body tingling in its fullness

Electrifying, no denying
The romance of Romeo and Juliet dying

DROWNING

Drowning under darkness
Sightless

Hair tangled, mangled
Weightless

I wouldn't ask but drowning
Is a disembodied frowning

I wouldn't ask but drowning
Is my plea

IT'S NOT

It's not the rain against my window
Or the voices in groups walking by

It's not my empty room
Or empty wine bottle
Or even empty bed

It's just
That I'm lonely

FAT CHANCE

Fat chance I have of marrying
Fat chance I have to wed
Fat chance I have of getting engaged
Or buying a double bed

Fat chance I have of dating
Fat chance of falling in love
Fat chance of receiving a tiny push
Or even a hefty shove

Fat chance of getting a boyfriend
Fat chance of going to dances
I'm through with men and marriage
And betting on all these fat chances!

WINDOWS OF PAIN

Criss-crosses pattern my brain
Reflected in windows of pane
They cross over again and again
These patterns made from the rain

2 A M

It's so quiet
Here in my kitchen
Alone
2am
But still I hear
Your breathing
Feel your fingers touch
Upon my neck
Feel your sharp intake
Of breath
Your lips pressed lightly
Against mine
Then fiercely possessing
My mouth
It is so very quiet
Here in my kitchen
So very alone
But still
I feel you

WITHIN MY GRASP

Imagine
Relaxing in a warm bath…

Imagine
Someone pulls the plug

TEARS ON AN UPTURNED CHEEK

Climb in bed beside me
And I can pretend you never left
Kiss my upturned cheek
And ignore the tears I wept

Turn your back and sleep
Forget the troubles that we share
And I can look at your innocent face
And fool myself you care

THE CANDLE

The candle basks your shadow
In a mellow, yellow glow
The dripping wax, the bluesy sax
It took a while to grow

The candle shining on your face
In a pale, frail light
Illuminating and understating
Deceiving me of sight

The candle melted to a stub
There was nothing I could do
No more wax, no more sax
And sadly no more you

THE WIND

Softly breathing
Cool, serene –
The wind
Presenting me
With a gift –
The man
Stormy passion
Strong, brave –
The man
Opening eyes
My dream becomes –
The wind

THE SMILE

The man afraid to smile
Afraid to stick around awhile

And yet when all was said and done
He wasn't fooling anyone

I thought I knew him well
But things as such are hard to tell

Too busy looking in his eyes
I missed the smile beyond the disguise

Sometimes I picture just his face
And see the smile so out of place

I wonder why he smiled at me
When I was just too blind to see

APPETITE

Such a large appetite
Do you really eat so much?
Judging by your bulge
I'd say it's all in your crotch

STAY AWHILE

Stay awhile and talk with me
And make me understand
Why I can kiss your lips
But cannot hold your hand

When you smile at me and hold me tight
I wish that I could see
If you just enjoy loving
Or if the joy is loving me

Why do you wait for me to find you?
Do I frighten you so much?
I don't want to keep you in a cage
I just want to feel your touch

Together we can have some fun
And I can make you understand
If all I can do is kiss your lips
I don't need to hold your hand

MOUTH TO MOUTH

Whilst catching all the flies
You fell into my mouth
I ate you
I think
You burned my tongue
And gave me an ulcer
But you tasted good
If I remember
I tried to spit you out
But it was too late
What we had together died
The minute I suffocated you
Restricted you
Smothered you
I don't think chewing on you helped either
So now you're gone and all I have left
Is a bitter taste in my mouth
Next time I'm looking alone and vulnerable
I'll keep my mouth shut

EXCLAMATION MARK

You break down my walls
Destroy my defences
And force me to cry

And as you cradle me in your arms
You wonder why

I hate you

TRAPPED

Like an animal in a cage
My confusion turns to rage

Tearing, scratching, biting
The futility of this fighting

Balancing on my wire
Escape is my desire

Escape

FRIEND OF MINE

To watch you laugh
At a joke that fell flat
The way you say
'I couldn't do that'

The way you tell me things
Straight from your heart
How you act dumb
To make others feel smart

When you tell me a joke
Punchline first
And I'm laughing so hard
I could burst

The way you stick by me
Time after time
I thank God
You're a good friend of mine

THE CACTUS

The cactus flower has no fears
And from its leaves it sheds no tears

No need for warmth or light or rain
The cactus simply feels no pain

Yet it can hurt if you should touch
It doesn't care for company much

To crack their shield is hard to do
The cactus is a lot like you

CLEANING LADIES HOOVERING

I'm sleeping in my big warm bed
I'm hearing a buzzing in my head
I open my eyes, the room is movering
Damn those cleaning ladies hoovering!

They move my things to a different corner
The telephone rings with another good morner
Don't they know that I've been boozering
Damn those cleaning ladies hoovering!

The later to bed, the earlier they ring
It's so annoying to have a cleaning lady sing
Perhaps they think the sound is soothering
Damn those cleaning ladies hoovering!

CANNIBALS

Cannibals eat human flesh
Tearing, ripping, slicing with ease
The smell of burning flesh
Wetting the tastebuds, ready to please

But they won't eat the brain
The head cut off and placed on a stake
Notice the bones stripped bare of the flesh
Easy to break

Cannibals eat humans they cannot differentiate
Between a chicken and a man
When they kill babies we find it barbaric
We'll stick to killing lambs

Cannibals used to eat humans
We've since killed them all

Naturally

BREATHING

Can I feel your breathing
Down my sleek and shiny spine
Waiting for the moment
When our bodies shall entwine

The passion simmers slowly
This desire's fit to burst
My body's burning up, oh!
I need to quench my thirst

The candle flickers enchantment
The pressure starts to climb
Can I feel your breathing
Or is it just mine

ALMOST

Cool candlelight
You fly-by-night
Sticky sweaty dusk
A gentle breeze
Your features freeze
The faint haunting smell of musk

Those watchful eyes
The starless skies
Moonlight by the sea
Flowers of pink
A fruity drink
Everything… but me

DANGEROUS

My love for you is dangerous
Seduction in deceit
Your fire keeps my body warm
Regardless of the 'heat'

Your crystal eyes and subtle strength
Send shivers down my spine
Each night I dream of your yielding arms
Always encircling mine

But my love for you is dangerous
You are not mine to hold
Though my body aches with burning desire
My sheets are always cold

When I'm in your arms embracing your warmth
All the dangers I dismiss
Through fear of detection or rejection and pain
I risk all for the touch of your kiss

BATED BREATH

I waited
With bated
Breath

I hated
You but with bated
Breath

I waited

Hating
This waiting
Breath not abating

Waiting
With bated
Breath

CAPTURED

Captured
I did not struggle
Within
My heart pounding
Wrists tied
Fingers tingling
I did not struggle
Throughout
For in a way I felt
Captured

CLOSE CONTACT

Catch me, I'm falling
Listen, I'm calling
Can you hear me?

Feel me come creeping
Watch as I'm weeping
Do you really fear me?

Strip me, I'm bare
It's not really fair
I just wanted you near me

FIND ME

You said I walked out of your life
Find me

You said I'd forget your name
Remind me

They say that love is blind
Blind me

Don't you know that I want you
To find me

BOX OF PLEASURES

I know
What you're looking for
But in this box of pleasures
I don't think you will find it

It's not that what you're after
Is unreachable
(Certainly not unpreachable)

But in this box of pleasures
There are better things
To find

CAN'T

Can't get you
Out of my mind

Hate the thought
Of leaving you behind

Can't get you

Hate the thought

Can't get the thought
Out of my mind

Hate you
Leaving me behind

Can't get you

Can't

WINDING MYSELF UP

Winding myself up
Winding myself down
Covering a smile
Erasing a frown

Turning my cheek
Covered in tears
Where will I be
In seventeen years

I'll be here on this spot
If not here in this town
Winding myself up
Winding myself down

UNDERSTANDING

If only someone
Understood

Why I feel
And what I touch

Understood
More than the why

Understood
Me

THAT WOULD BE TELLING

You ask me why I party
When everyone's asleep
You wonder at my motive
And the hours that I keep

I offer you a deal
And you ask me what I'm selling
I'd really like to tell you
But then that would be telling

You ask me why I'm leaving
Is it something that you said
I notice that you say it
From the comfort of your bed

You tell me that you love me
And then you start your yelling
Of course I'd like to tell you
Alas, that would be telling

WALK THE STREETS

Walk the streets at night
Lonely and confused
Waking in the morning light
Mind and body fused

Walk the streets at night
Do so every year
And every night I cry in fright
What am I doing here?

TRYING TO CRY

I know you've been out in the rain
I know it's been causing you pain

To see all that water flow free
To know that it's still hurting me

The tears that you cried were in vain
I just think you've been out in the rain

THE LADY KILLER

She likes to stab and shoot you down
When you smile, she likes to frown

She's poison and she'll cut your throat
In your sea of troubles she'll sink your boat

Although you find her such a thrill
Beware, the lady likes to kill

THE WANT AD

Lazy days, intimate chat
Challenging tone: can you improve that?

Apply in writing; do it today
If you've nothing to lose and have plenty to say

Looking for fun; no strings attached
Man needs woman imperfectly matched

Well, I answered the ad; it was all a good joke
And you turned out to be a fun-loving bloke

But our time is limited, like the hourglass sand
And there's just one thing I don't understand

If you don't need a woman to share your life
(And that's not to imply that I want to be wife)

If you want me one minute but just not the next
(I hope I'm not reading this out of context)

Then why am I here, free of all ties
And why, my friend, did you advertise?

THE AFFAIR

Judging by the way you stare
You think I have a secret
But honestly I've never seen him before
The fact that we talked
And exchanged a smile
Means nothing
Anyway
I stopped loving you
A long time ago

WET CURTAIN

Behind the shower curtain
Is a tap
And as the curtain rises
We all clap

When the water falls
We close our eyes
After the curtain calls
We slowly rise

Turning off the tap
The curtain soaks
Leaving the auditorium
We don our cloaks

The curtain frames the stage
The scene is set
But you shouldn't be surprised
If the curtain's wet

SOMEONE MUST CARE

If all the lonely hearts
Lived very near
And someone cried out
Wouldn't somebody hear?

If all the lonely hearts
Were gathered collectively
And somebody smiled
Wouldn't somebody see?

For all the lonely hearts
Breathing the same air
If someone saw all these lonely hearts
Then someone must care

QUIETLY

Quietly I let myself in
You could have heard the drop of a pin

Turning, I bolted the door
And moved silently across the tile floor

Standing, surveying my gloom
Moonlight splashing the room

Sleeping, his face dark and dull
Swiftly the crack of a skull

Never had time for a shout
Quietly I let myself out

SO EASY

Like putty in my hands
I squidge you through my thumb
As I mould your subtle outline
Your feelings become numb
And even when I called you
I didn't think you'd come
So easy

Like dirt beneath my feet
I wipe my shoes so clean
In all the time I trampled
You didn't think me mean
When I return from hunting
You don't care where I've been
So easy

I knew I had you captive
You couldn't get away
But like putty in my hands
I felt you turn to clay
And when you turned and left me
It was I who felt betray
So easy

POISON

Too busy guzzling
Into my neck nuzzling

Took the bottle, opened the cap
Did you think I fell into your lap?

Drinking your fill your lips you moisten
But you didn't read the label it said I was poison

SILENT SHOES

My silent shoes on the hollow ground
Step so light they make hardly a sound

I stand on the pavement, neck craned high
Stare through your window and heave a sigh
And wonder, yes, I wonder why

My silent shoes with nary a sound
Always walk on this hollow ground

PHOENIX

In the dawn I recovered
Rising from the ashes
I knew, long before you did

Perhaps just a memory
Imagined in haste
But I doubt it

Would you care to partake in a trial of your own
Or maybe you think I'm just bluffing
Maybe I am, in a strange sort of way

SITTING

Sitting
Thinking
Pondering
Waiting
Wishing
I were somewhere else

KNIFE

I saw you pick up the knife
And wondered what you would do
I noticed that the knife
Seemed alien to you

Your eyes seemed not to see
Such a wicked instrument
As you turned your face away
Across the knife you leant

Yes, I saw you pick up the knife
And I watched you turn the blade
Saw you pierce the tender skin
And the patterns that it made

I watched without regret
Though I was sure you were in pain
My eyes displayed no fear
And your expression was the same

I should have tried to stop you
For it robbed you of your life
But I was mesmerised by your action
And it was such a pretty knife

JUST BEGINNING

Just beginning, not too fast
Nothing wrong with starting last

Just beginning, it's kind of fun
To be just beginning when everyone's done

PAST TENSE

You were the sort of friend
Only good people deserve
Is that why I lost you?

I made a mistake
I thought I didn't need you
I was so wrong

I'm sorry for the pain
But now I know how it feels
I miss you

More than you'll ever know

I'VE COME THIS FAR

Can't believe I've come this far
So hard, so long
Looking back at all the tears
I know my destination can't be wrong

But when I see you standing on your own
Staring for so long
This sadness deep inside of me
Forces me to stay so strong

Can't believe I've come this far
After all your efforts of attack
But you'd better believe this time
That for me there'll be no turning back

CUT THE CAKE

It's not until you cut the cake
That you realise your age
As you blow out all the candles
You think it's just a stage

But the frustration of those wasted years
Soon will turn to rage
And by the time you see your fate
You're trapped behind your cage

Your life reveals an open book
And as you turn the page
It's not until you cut the cake
That you realise your age

ELIMINATION

If we eliminate the spontaneity
We are left with the plan
By removing the psychosomatics
We are faced with the man

Catching a cold
Is an easier skill
When one becomes weak
You move in for the kill

If you don't know the answer
The question remains
When you do know the answer
The question's the same

FREEDOM

His wild hair flowing
Majestically in the wind
Those fiery eyes expressing
His independent mind

The raised head sniffing
Triumphantly in the air
High atop a mountain
Alone with no one there

Sheer black hoof raised
Ready to squash an enemy
Wild and free and noble
Able to be what he wants to be

The strong black stallion
Rearing upon both hinds
Alive and fiercely living
Free within my mind

I TRIED

Congested feelings
Flailing through my fingertips
I tried
Someone said I cried

Head and shoulders reeling
Finally the closing of our lips
I cried
Someone said I tried

Would it have mattered terribly if I had lied
The love I gave never would have died
Except you knew that I had lied

Forgotten feelings
Licked between my lips
I cried
Someone said I lied

But by your feet as I lay kneeling
Your hair playing through my fingertips
I cried
At least I think I tried

I CRIED

When you left I cried
It felt as though my heart had died
You said you loved me but you lied
When you left I cried and cried

AROMATIC

Like a favourite fragrance
Your scent will linger on
If I don't protect my bottle
Your scent will soon be gone

If I use it up too quickly
You simply overpower
If I use your contents wisely
You will blossom like a flower

I cannot break your bottle
You're simply much too clever
For whilst the bottle disappears
The scent stays on forever

DID YOU KNOW

Did you know that your lying and sneaking
And pretending you were sleeping
Was never disguise for me
I knew that you cheated
I knew you had lied
But when you left me crying
Wishing you were lying
Knowing that in all this time
You'd never known
Did you know
That I loved you

CONSIDERING

Considering how busy you are
Shouldn't I be grateful
That you think of me at all
Considering what a great guy you are
Shouldn't I be thankful
That you even bother to call

Considering how you break our dates
Shouldn't I realise
That to you I'm no big deal
For someone so considerate
Shouldn't you consider
How I feel

CRAZY

Crazy, they said to me
I thought they were talking about you
As they closed the iron bars
And I saw you through the grills
I felt so sorry for your depressing captivity
But as you turned your back and walked away
I saw my four walls and knew

HELLO

Hello
I saw you standing there
Looking so alone
I thought I'd introduce myself
Even though you're on the phone

Hello
I like the look of you
There's something in your eyes
It's nice to see you talking
Although you're full of lies

Hello
Now please don't walk away
There's more to me, you know
But before you get the best of me
You will have to say hello

COLLAPSING IN A HEAP

My head keeps screaming
Is this real or am I dreaming

When I look in the mirror I'm always frowning
Deep inside I know I'm drowning

Have you ever cried without shedding a tear?
Can't seem to control my rising fear

I look a mess, I feel despair
I want to escape but I don't know where

Why do I show you these words that I write?
Am I asking for help or do I just want a fight?

On the surface, with effort, I try to pretend
Like a wound cut too deep, I can't seem to mend

This self-destruction is hard to resist
But if I don't, deep inside, I'll no longer exist

I ONCE HAD A DREAM

I once had a dream
That could carry me away
Dispel all my realities
And pains of yesterday

I thought about it always
Whenever I was blue
My spirit soared and I adored
A dream that could come true

How could such a wishful dream
Suddenly disappear
To reach out and there's nothing
To touch, to taste, to hear

I once had a dream
A promise of things to come
I once had a dream
Now I have none

COUNT YOURSELF LUCKY

Count yourself lucky
That I wasn't home
Coz if I had known
That you didn't phone
I'd have dropped you

Count yourself lucky
I can't read what you write
Coz if I had been right
And you were out again last night
I'd have dropped you

Count yourself lucky
That you dropped me today
That you were able to have your say
Coz if I had had my own way
I'd have dropped you anyway

CATCHING MY BREATH

Don't worry about the rest
I'm just catching my breath
Letting you pass
But chasing your shadow
Caught in the crossroads
I'm lost
But believe me
I'm paying the cost
Don't worry, I'm just
Catching my breath

FRIENDSHIP

You do nothing like I want things to be done
So I think you have defied me

You force me to live my life on my own
So I feel you have betrayed me

Just when I think you're rejecting my friendship
You reach out and touch me

So maddening to have no control, no possession
To not be able to take until you have given

I swear I will not chase you,
Crave you,
Need you

I will reject you,
Abandon you,
Ignore you

And then…
You reach out
And I hold your hand

COLLECTIBLE PIECES

Collectible pieces
Nephews and nieces

Student in jeans
White limousines

Porcelain dolls
Shoes without soles

Questions and answers
Pink ballet dancers

Stallions and mares
Underground fares

Dolphins in water
The hand of your daughter

Making love by the sea
Bread and jam served with tea

Snow white as fleeces
Collectible pieces

CHILD'S PLAY

Daddy bought me a budgie
Blue with a *yellow* chest
My brother also had one
But I liked my budgie best

She would fly around her cage
Tweetering all the day
I would rush straight home from school
Just so we could play

Then somehow she got sick
So we took her to the vet
They didn't like her chances
But it wasn't over yet

Daddy took me home again
And said I had to wait
And when he finally brought her home
I thought she looked just great

Yes, I love my little budgie
I love my budgie best
She is such a lovely *yellow*
With a beautiful *blue* chest

A COUGH

A cough caught in my throat
A heel caught in my grate
This temporary imprisonment
Just hates to wait

This window in my bedroom
Always sheds new light
Just waiting for the darkness
Is like welcoming the night

A cough caught in my throat
Makes my breathing ill-at-ease
But if I swallow
Will the cough become disease?

BUT WHEN

But when I opened the door
You were there

But when I called
You came

Who cares
What other people say

When I opened the door
You were there

CATCHING UP WITH YOU

You said you didn't want me
Things would never be the same
And I knew this was the last time
You would ever speak my name

You were thinking of your future
I was caught up in the past
I couldn't keep up with you
You were moving much too fast

I watched you dating other girls
Like a voyeur through the pane
Your life was full of sunshine
Whilst I stood in the rain

But lately you've been changing
Things aren't going quite so well
Your life is sad and lonely
Just like an empty shell

But I'm busy with my own life
My lonely nights are few
And after all those years of chasing
I'm finally catching up with you

WOMANLY VIEWS

I flatly refuse
To be abused
So you should be amused
To find that I use
My womanly views
To take what I choose
I'm giving no clues
On the don't-s and the do-s
Just hope I don't lose
These womanly views

THE LION

You'll never know these feelings
Hidden deep within my eyes
The secrets I'm revealing
Are just a thin disguise

But in my world of fantasy
The lion leaves his lair
And as my dream became reality
I saw you standing there

THE GAME

I don't seem fussed
So you call this lust
I trust
You have me sussed

So how can you not see
The fire burning inside of me

I'll play the game and count the scores
For unless the lion roars
My presence here will be no more

THREE LITTLE WORDS

How can I say those three little words
In such a way you'll believe me
How can I capture your roaming heart
In a way that you'll never deceive me

All that I've wanted is shining in you
Yet you doubt me and cast me aside
You still hold me close and hug me tight
But what are you feeling inside

And I've tried really hard to remain close to you
But whatever I do you don't care
And I know that one day when I open my eyes
You'll no longer be standing there

SOMEHOW

Something went wrong
Somewhere along the way
I never meant to fall for you
I never meant to stay

I pretended it was nothing
But who am I trying to kid
I never meant to fall for you
But somehow I did

YOU FOLLOW

It doesn't matter where I go
You follow

Once, every time I turned around
You were there

In my heart, my mind, the memories
Linger still

It doesn't matter where I go
You follow

YOU LET ME GO

Smiling at your moody face
Trying to look my best
Hoping that by staying
You'd forget about the rest

Doing everything the way you want
Saying nothing much at all
Smiling and always hoping
That you won't forget to call

Loving every moment
But my happiness won't last
This time we have together
Is fading much too fast

It's not the fact you're leaving
It's what you wanted, this I know
It's just how easily it ended
And the way you let me go

NO MORE

Can't you tell
I know you well
I've seen this game before
You ask for none
I give you some
And then you ask for more

The problem is
With all this biz
I'm getting pretty bored
I'm sick of hearing
Whilst you're leering
Of the many times you've scored

So I suggest
That you get dressed
And take yourself elsewhere
Coz I've had enough
So I'm calling your bluff
For I no longer care

SCATTER

Scatter
Said the catter
Ratter tatter tat
Take that you dirty rat
Take that
The latter
In the hatter (felt)
Wiped his feet upon the mat
The catter
Didn't matter
With his ratter tatter tat
For the latter
(Who was fatter)
Had a laugh about the matter
Turning to the catter
Said, you missed

TRAFFIC JAMS

Traffic jams
Vehicle crams
Swearings and damns
In these traffic jams

Faces overeating
Engines overheating
Hands on wheels a-beating
Voices like sheep bleating

Youngsters playing Wham!
Bumpers start to ram
Play it again, Sam
I'm in a traffic jam

THE DREAM

I close my eyes and sleep
And whilst you watch
The rise and fall of my chest
I dream
Transported into fantasy
I picture your sweet head
Resting upon a soft, white cloud
As you softly sleep
You dream
Such dreams so pure and fragile
Bind together a love
That permeates the dream
And creates
Life

WORDS WORTH

Failure
Infidelity
Past
Liberated
Scared
Fast

You
Maybe
Me
Hope
Care
Free

THE CRUEL AND CUNNING SUB-PLOT

Cunning how they twisted
In the heat, blistered

Sedentary on the ledge
Yet silent in their pledge

The French-grey petals frowning
Crumpets for breakfast browning

Crackling in the wicker-chair
Curtains flutter in mid-air

The perfect scene for Sunday brunch
But then there comes the crunch

The bloody stain from bullet to head
And the body decomposing on the bed

HOW COME

How come I can't look at you
But always turn away
And every time you visit
I wish that you would stay

How come I can feel you
Although we never touch
We're not often in the same room
But I enjoy our time so much

But the most maddening thing of all
Hidden in my shelf
Although I won't admit it to your face
Why can't I to myself?

SOMEDAY

Someday I'll wait for you
But not today
For some reason my presence
Is forcing you to stay
One day when you're leaving me
You can guarantee I'll say
That I will wait for all eternity
For you someday

WASTED

Wasted feelings
Lap upon the shore
I lost my chance
I can't feel them anymore

Wait for me
Just around the bend
I'd have been there sooner
But this road will never end

THE COMMUTER

I am not a daredevil
Waiting to be seen
I drive on through the traffic lights
Because they're mostly green

I slow down at a corner
Only if I wish to turn
I'm really not responsible
If my motor likes to burn

I drive at breakneck speed
Because that is the limit
And if you think my light's too bright
Just tell me and I'll dim it

I honk my horn and shake my fist
Merely to attract
For I'm just a normal motorist
And that, my dear, is fact

ALRIGHT

Alright I am tired
I am bored
The traffic lights
Are amber, green and red

But imagine how bored I'd be
If I were dead

REVENGE

I know how much you hurt me
In your despising little way
The lies that you delivered
And all the petty things you'd say

I know you thought I'd let you
Smear my name into the dirt
But you misjudged the way I'm feeling
And the degree that I've been hurt

I vowed I'd never let you leave
But I suppose you hadn't heard
And now as I stare upon your grave
Revenge is such an understated word

SABOTAGING SUBMARINES

This is serious
Commander Spick declared
Enemy subs approaching
We must bewared
Scramble on deck, serious
I am feeling scared
Enemy subs approaching
Commander Spick has stared
Telescope up, he booms
Eyes through glasses peered
Eyes and telescope contact
Eyes no longer paired
Enemy subs, Spick spits
I wonder how they fared
These enemy subs approaching
I wonder how they dared
Commander Spick spots trouble
Me, I'm no longer thered
Enemy subs contact
Holes in subs well aired
Commander Spick can't swim
Me no longer cared
Me no longer breathing
Nothing more be said

SO BLUE

So blue
Contrast to the land
So blue
Walking hand in hand

So blue
The sky robbed me of you
But I'll always remember your eyes
So blue

PARTING WORDS

I don't have much to give you
Though you know I'd give it all
This friendship formed between us
Could break down any wall

Emotions don't mean anything
Emitted from cold lips
I prefer to taste my champagne
By taking slower sips

I don't have much to give you
You seem to take much less
As opposed to taking all your love
I prefer a sweet caress

I don't have much to give you
But know that whilst apart
This poem that I give you
Is really just the start

LOOKING AT YOU LOOKING AT ME

You wear mirrored glasses
Though the sun will shine no more
Looking at you looking at me
Wondering what it's all for

Looking at you I can't help remembering
The rise before the fall
Looking at me no longer feeling the same
Why do we look at all?

SALLY WENT DOWN TO THE RIVER

Sally went down to the river to swim
Sally went down but couldn't get in

Water is cold, yabbies is yuck
Crabs bite, leeches suck

Sally came up from the river for tea
Nobody home but Sally and me

LISTENING

Listening is not half as bad as
Hearing
The words you say
Are like arrows through my heart
Bleeding
Me dry
My eyes
So blinded
But who needs to be reminded
Not listening
Just may well be the start

IF I COULD

If I could paint a picture
I'd paint one of you
If I could make a seat
I'd build it for two
If I could write a song
I'd sing it to you
If I could write a mystery
You'd be the clue
If I could marry a millionaire
What would I do?
I'd give up all that money
If I could be with you

I HAVE SEEN THOSE EYES BEFORE

I have seen those eyes before
Staring from behind the persecuted
Pleading from beneath a withered brow
Fired up in a young man's anger

I have seen those eyes before
Fleetingly in the executed
Harmlessly in the young
Finally in my reflection

I have seen those eyes before

I DON'T WANT TO SAY GOODBYE

If you wonder why I'm sad
Or cling to you like mad

If you wonder why I'm evasive
And find your actions so pervasive

It's simply because
I don't want to say goodbye

I CAN LET GO NOW

So many summers
Struggling to survive
Crippled by disease
Barely keeping you alive

I, too, was old and tired
Ready to let go
But I couldn't bear to leave you
And I couldn't tell you so

You didn't want to burden
Even though you were in pain
I talked you out of dying
I must have been insane

My appearance became weary
Heaven knows my body tried
But you didn't ask the reason
If you had, I would have lied

When you finally gave up fighting
Well I muddled on somehow
But now that you are gone, my dear
I can finally let go now

CARRIED ME AWAY

Carried me away

Memories of a happier day
What else could I say
It just seemed like yesterday

Carried me away

The games we used to play
Wishing you would stay
For just another day

Carried me far away…

BUT YOU

Empty bed but you
Inside my head you knew

Wishing well, flooded emotion
Enough to fill the entire ocean
The seagull has such devotion

I flew the distance expecting nothing
But you

CALLING

Calling
Tumbling over obstacles, scratches
Pretending to be
Falling
Maybe one day…
Maybe one day…
Maybe never
Won't I ever learn
Stalling
Oh, always, always, don't care if I wait forever
Wish I could stop this
Bawling
Baby it's a heartache turning on the water
Washing clean
Sprawling
Across white sheets, mansion in the countryside
Can't you hear me
Calling

TORN APART

Torn apart, the scars laid bare
I hate waking up with nobody there

Left alone, I miss you so much
Crying out for your tender touch

SOMETIMES

Sometimes
In my darkness
I wish I could stop aching
For you

Sometimes
I wish I could stop whispering
Your name

Sometimes
I wonder aloud
How much longer
Can I stand it
How much longer

But I always
Ache for you

Always
Whisper your name

Never
Wonder aloud

SOMETHING WICKED

The wicked walk so quickly
Feet hardly strike the ground
With every strike of footstep
Comes the wicked, I have found

The wicked know the footsteps
Be they heavy, be they light
Never strike a footstep
When out walking in the night

For if walking in the moonlight
You find feet that strike the ground
It is sure that in this moonlight
Something wicked you have found

REMEMBER MY FACE

Study my face for a long, long time
Remember the face you saw was mine

Then when I'm gone and you're thinking of me
Remember my face and maybe you'll see

Maybe you'll see the tears in my eyes
The pain in my face as we say our goodbyes

The hurt that I felt as you walked out the door
Remember my face for you'll see it no more

PREPARED

No one prepared me for you
I tried to play it smooth
But despite all the men I played
None prepared me for you

LOOKING

Ten to eleven
News bulletin
Cat goes out
Late train home
Curtains parted

I'm looking out

Ten to twelve
Movie over
Cat comes in
Last train home
Curtains drawn

I'm looking in

Ten to one
Television off
Cat asleep
No trains running
You're not home

Looking away

DOESN'T MATTER

Doesn't matter
Anymore
I whispered
To the closing door

I LET THE PHONE RING

I let the phone ring
With a shaking hand and aching heart
I reached out
But felt only the coldness

I let the phone ring
Each ring piercing through my heart
Each one tearing me apart
The gap widened
I reached out
But felt only the distance

I let the phone ring
But your patience had worn thin
This distance was too great
Your heart could not wait
I listened into silence
And cradled the coldness in my heart

ALWAYS

I always caught the twelve-o-nine
Always furnished rooms with pine
Always slept upon my spine
Always

I always took you out to dine
Always bought the best of wine
Always poured first yours not mine
Always

I always said you looked just fine
Always wore my Calvin Kleins
Always drew the bottom line
Always

I always picked you up on time
Always picked the grapes off vines
Always picked a verse that rhymes
Always

A DAY

As if listening
To every word you say
A day without you
Is just another day

SECRET MISSION

Softly now, our toes are tipped
Keep it quiet, mouth tightly lipped
Oh, be careful, someone tripped
We're on a secret mission

We're going on a journey long
There are four of us and we're all quite strong
And if things should go horribly wrong
We've got our television

So keep it hush, we're on our way
We haven't really got all day
Where we're headed, no one can say
But we're on a secret mission

GETTING INTO MISCHIEF

I like being five years old
And running through the house
I like scaring Mummy
When I show her my pet mouse
And I like making mud pies
Coz I think they taste real grouse
But most of all
I like getting into mischief
I like telling Daddy
That his car has hit a tree
And I like falling over
Coz then Mummy kisses me
I *don't* like my little brother
Because he's only three
But most of all
I like getting into mischief
I like playing chasey
Because I like to run
I like doing things
That no one else has done
And I like all my friends
I think they're lots of fun
Because most of all
They like getting into mischief

WATCH ME

Watch me, I can tumble
Watch me, Mamma, stumble

Pick me up and cuddle
Drop me in a puddle

Very deep and dark
I can play in the park

I can play
Every day

Watch me, Mamma,
Watch me

Watch me jump and hop
Watch me, I can't stop

Watch me

THE BOSS

It's totally preposterous
I'm sure you will agree
When the boss gives you dictation
With his hand upon your knee

And the problem with his desk
Is no matter how athletic you may feel
It's hard to run around it
With the boss hot on your heel

And he's oh so understanding
When you start to feel the stress
But it's hard to keep from stressing
When his hand is down your dress

And when he asks you to work overtime
And you both are left alone
It's a worry to discover
That he disconnects the phone

And it's hard to tell the staff
That you still must call him Sir
When your birthday gift becomes
A coat made out of fur

When your day consists of locking doors
And drawing curtains tight
And making sure the order
Of your clothes are looking right

When you're never doing typing
But you're always getting praises
For hard work that is rewarded
With holidays and raises

Then perhaps the office gossip
Isn't really so far-fetched
When they say that your devotion to your boss
Is somewhat stretched

For it's hard, they say, to justify
The good things in your life
When your boss only takes advantages
Because you are his wife!

THE RECEPTIONIST

Somebody asked for the tall one
But I said you were out to tea
Somebody rang for the smart one
But I thought they were talking about me

Somebody asked for the pain in the bum
But you were engaged on the phone
Somebody asked for that outrageous one
But I told them you had gone home

Somebody asked for the stunning one
But I knew they didn't want you
Then somebody asked for the dumb, ugly one
So, honey, I'm putting them through!

THE JOYS

Monday I was suicidal
Tuesday comatose
Wednesday brought a bout of blues
Thursday was just gross

Friday perked me up a bit
Saturday I slept
Sunday moped about the house
Monday I just wept

The days don't really matter
The mood swings just the same
Sometimes I cope quite easily
At times I go insane

I pondered on my feelings
And wondered if just maybe
It's attributed to the fact
That I've just had a baby

TEMP

I am a temp which means quite a lot
Sometimes I'm busy and sometimes I'm not

Sometimes it's boring, well *most* of the time
But a Temp doing nothing is a hell of a crime

I have x-ray vision so I know who is here
Unreadable writing? I find it perfectly clear

No need to explain what to do, where to go
I'm a Temp you see so I already know

Yes, a Temp means a lot, the job has its perks
Even though at times I'm surrounded by jerks

And I *always* have plenty of work to be done
Like what? Well, like typing this poem for one!

MY BOSS

My boss wants his coffee so I jump
I try to put in poison but it lumps

I try to add more sugar but there's none left
I try to spill it on him but he's too deft

I put in a scorpion, a quick and easy kill
But the coffee's too hot and it won't stay still

So I guess I'll be making coffee til I'm old
With ant-infested sugar and water that is cold

MY FRIDGE

There was no lettuce in my fridge
Just a patch of slime
I wondered where my lettuce went
And why this slime was lime

Another day I discovered
A pool of vivid red
My tomatoes had gone missing
And the kids had not been fed

Things were so peculiar
And we suffered in our grief
For a fridge containing liquid
With a bucket underneath

But things did not end there
It was getting out of hand
For next morning was a pool of white
Where once my fridge did stand

OLD AND PEELING

These walls are old and peeling
This heart's taking a long time healing

Sitting alone, this place is a mess
Did I think it would make the pain hurt less?

I stare at your picture, my heart fills with feeling
But I know that the walls remain old and peeling

TOO FAST

This carnival atmosphere
Is really a joke
You can't see the fire
For fear of the smoke

You're laughing too loudly
To notice my tears
I can't keep relating
To all of your fears

You're running too fast
You give me a stitch
I call you a dreamer
You call me a bitch

All of these matters
Are better just dropped
For you're moving too quickly
To notice I've stopped

FIGHTERS

Their injuries are inside them
The fight at times absurd
Is not fought with fists of iron
But with the spoken word

It's just the way they are
Addicted to love and war
And they wouldn't fight so hard
If each weren't worth fighting for

The trouble is it has to end
As thy bitter enemy and not thy friend

BLANK

Blank pages firmly shut
No ink to bleed
Along the margins
If thoughts produced more colour
I could read
But I can't

A LITTLE POEM

I'd write a little poem
But the words won't rhyme
It always seems to happen
Almost every time

There's nothing I can do
There's very little doubt
I simply have no clue
What this poem's all about

I guess I should write one
But there's very little point
I end up with a headache
And my fingers out of joint

Something just compels me
Though I don't know what to say
But what bothers me the most
Is why you read it anyway

A LIFE SO BLEAK AND DULL

Can anyone imagine
A life so bleak and dull
She wakes up in the morning
A throbbing in her skull

She tries to do her make-up
But she hasn't got a clue
She tries colour in her wardrobe
But is always dressed in blue

The car stalls every morning
And usually at the lights
The lift is always crowded
So she walks the seven flights

Her office is so boring
Her furniture so old
And though she has a heater
Her room is always cold

She often spills her coffee
As she stumbles down the hall
And when she's feeling poorly
No one notices at all

Her in-tray's over-flowing
Her out-tray non-existent
And the office leech ignores her
Though with others he's persistent

When at five the office empties
She is always working late
It doesn't seem to matter
For she never has a date

Her car stalls yet again
In the dark and in the rain
The mechanics never come
They know it's her again

Her flat is cramped and dirty,
The air is dry and stuffy
But it doesn't make a difference
No one drops in for a coffee

Stuck her head into the oven
With intention there to kill
But the gas was disconnected
For she hadn't paid the bill

So she lives a life of boredom
With no relief in sight
From her working in the office
To her stalling at the lights

And though of all her problems
You will never hear her speak
Can anyone imagine
A life so dull and bleak

CATCHING RAINDROPS

Catching raindrops through dry lips
Feel them fall from frozen fingertips

When did I stop feeling the pain
Was I always this way, or did I change
Now I like to stand out in the rain
Tell me, do you think that's strange

Swimming naked through a sea of blood
With feet bogged down in mud

You know if I was free, I could fly
I bet you're thinking I'm deranged
You know I don't even know why
I thought that things had changed

ALL IT TAKES

It only takes one crack in the sidewalk

To grow a flower
Think of all that power

One bends, one breaks
And that's all it takes

THE TRUTH

Jokes aren't funny
Until you laugh
No one looks good
In a photograph

Side-saddle is senseless
Unless you wear skirts
And they're right
Love hurts

NEW AGE

Can you feel the dance
The music slow and steady
Can you hear the chant
The voices strong and ready

Can you see the spirit
Soaring straight and true
Can you know the truth
Can you?

VOICES

When words were spoken upon the ground
Many heard the solemn sound

They listened softly with eyes to the sky
And believed that they could truly fly

When words were spoken to the spirit within
Our souls felt the awakening begin

And as the words through our mouths emerged
We heard the voices as they converged

The spoken words now fully grown
With a voice we recognised as our own

THE BEGINNING

It's the beginning
No second coming
No end of the world
No blind leading the blind
The beginning
The understanding
The remembering
All the answers are within
And so as you begin
The world shifts and tilts
And straightens up again
And what was once awry
Becomes clearly even
And even you are clear
You remember
You understand
And joyfully
Peacefully
And excitedly
You begin

EARTH

Seeing the calmness of the eagle
Spreading its wings across the land
Feeling the earth so warm and heavy
Falling softly through my hands

Hearing the water flowing smoothly
And the birds sing in the trees
Feeling the sunshine warm my shoulders
And my hair lift in the breeze

Knowing that all this earth is with me
Each and every day
Filling my life with joy and meaning
In a million different ways

Wake to the sunrise, end with a sunset
Watching the rain cleanse and renew
I can see all these many treasures
So tell me, why can't you?

THE DANCE

Rattlesnake sound, soft earth
The dance begins

Treading lightly, moving slowly
Many voices like thunder
Many footsteps growing faster
The dance has begun

Feel the strength
We are here

SADNESS IS A LONELY ROOM

Sadness is a lonely room
Tears a river flowing
Hope is where you plant the seed
And see a flower growing

I can see the sunshine
Warm a tired tree
Spread the branches far and wide
For all the world to see

Sadness is a lonely thought
The room is in your mind
Turn the key and enter
And happiness you'll find

A NEW DAY

The summer breeze gently lifts my spirit
The cooling waters cleanse my mind
And all the while my hopes
Instead of scattering in the wind
Are planting in the earth
Soon to grow and prosper
With the sun's warmth
The summer breeze
The cooling waters
And the earth's hope
I will be one again
In mind and spirit

THE TRUTH WITHIN

Open your mind and see the truth
Believing is the only proof

What's real is all that's in your mind
What you feel is what you find

Separates the fact from fiction
Believing in your own conviction

If it goes against the grain
It's only going to cause you pain

Listen to your inner voice
When you're forced to make a choice

Live your life true and kind
And believe the truth is in your mind

STRENGTH

The strength lies within
Where truth is clear and real
Where quietly you listen
To how you really feel

You are stronger than you imagine
More healthy than you know
What happens on the outside
You can easily let go

Let pain and heartache fade away
The important thing is knowing
You are the strength within
Protecting, nurturing, growing

INNER VOICE

In the quiet of your mind
Hear the voice within
At first it may be a whisper
Barely audible
And easily ignored
The doubts erase it
Or the ego overrides it
Until one day the voice
Grows stronger
And questions asked
Are answered
And when those around you envy
Your belief in yourself
You wonder why
They just don't listen
To the inner voice
Within

LIFE

Under my tree a bird lay crying
I gently crushed the grass
And pushed the air
And watched the bird fly
The fallen tears
Watered the earth
And my tree grew taller
The bird returned
And sat on the highest branch
I listened to the birdsong
Shaded by my tree
And breathed the fresh air
I felt the warmth
Smelt the spring
And saw the miracle
Of life

A RAY OF HOPE

In the grey gloom
In a darkened room

In the deepest hole
In my very soul

The sky turns blue
And the sun shines through

And fills up the hole
In my very soul

PRAYERS ANSWERED

She was crying softly
In the very back row
Of a rather elaborate church

The worshippers sang hymns
And basked in their own complacency
The priest stood at the altar
And rather grandly boomed humility and grace

And all the while she sat
In the very back row
Crying softly

As the singing reached a crescendo
And the priest nodded oh so sagely
She felt an unseen hand lightly touch her
And an unheard voice whisper
You have been heard

The priest stood at the altar
The worshipers prayed
And she sat
In the very back row

NOT LONG AGO

My grandmother died
Not long ago
Mixed with relief (for she was in pain)
Was the grief and sadness
I would not be seeing her again
It would be nice to have her here
With me
For though the years may pass
And I become accustomed
To not having her around
It will always seem to me
That my grandmother passed away
Not long ago

DISABLED VIEWS

A perfect child is born
But the adults cannot see
Their vision is distorted
By the fantasy

The perfect child is seen
In the fractured light
And the view that they regard
As not quite right

Is the reflection of the truth
As it smiled
To let the mother finally see
Her perfect child

AS ONE

I stood alone in a rainforest
And heard the whispers start
Tranquillity surrounded me
And touched upon my heart

I heard the same sweet voices
As by the sea I stood
And as my spirit soared so free
I finally understood

It was as though the voices whispering
Were actually my own
The earth, fire, water, air
Were saying welcome home

SECRET MISSION - REVISED

Softly now, our toes are tipped
Keep it quiet, mouth tightly lipped
Oh, be careful, someone tripped
We're on a secret mission

We're going to a forest deep
Where fire-breathing dragons sleep
And in their cave they like to keep
A witch and a magician

So to the rescue we shall go
Searching for them high and low
Make sure the dragons never know
Shh! We're on a secret mission

Through the trees, across the lake
Oh no, the dragons are awake
What an awful noise they make
Now they know our secret mission

We'll have to sneak around the back
And make it a surprise attack
We'll hide the witch in a magic sack
And rescue the magician

Then when the dragons are asleep
Through the cave we'll softly creep
Keep it quiet, not a peep
We've been on a secret mission!

MORE THAN THIS

There must be something more than this
But I cannot say what that is

To stare at spaces on the wall
And nothing comprehends at all

To live a life day in, day out
With nothing much to talk about

Yet somehow something feels amiss
There must be more to life than this

BREATHTAKING EVIDENCE

Capturing my imagination
With the stillness of the wind
It's a magical emotion
Of the mind
But I know the secret
Of the movement within
It's another reason
To believe imagination
Wonder what it means
When they say
We are not alone

SHADOWS

Shadows in the night
Tricks of the mind
Searching around corners
For the love you left behind

Waiting for the day
When my memories will fade
And all the time wishing
You had stayed

DUNGEON

I ask my sister Jenny
For a word to write a rhyme
It has to be a good one
But I don't have that much time

I want to make it witty
And I want to make it good
And it has to be a simple one
So it's easily understood

Jenny gives the word
And I start to pen the prose
It isn't very easy
When you don't know how it goes

I write a couple of verses
I finish it and then
I present it to my sister
Saying, 'Here, it's done, Jen.'
(Dungeon)

AUCTION

On a windy day in a tree-lined street
Stood a handsome house, quiet and neat
The milling crowd shuffled their feet
As they stood on the curb in the gentle heat

In a tree-lined street on a windy day
As an Auctioneer sized up who could pay
The money makers came out to play
And a sad, old man turned and walked away

MY NAME IS MUD

When I was just a little boy
My parents named me Bud

Until I struck out with the girls
And they renamed me Dud

I went to war as a killing machine
My nickname then was Blood

Back home my emotional dam had burst
And the girls, they called me Flood

A powerful man, I had an affair
The tabloids dubbed me Stud

My girlfriend left a note on the door
It said, 'I'm leaving, Crud'

As I grew older and shrivelled up
The young ones called me Spud

Until I died and was buried deep
And now my name is Mud

TRUE LOVE

I heard the whispers in my head
But by then my heart was dead

A voice so soft and pure of heart
But still it ripped my soul apart

For I could not hear love so kind
When to my heart my soul was blind

A tragic love had wounded deep
And so my soul I prayed to keep

Emotions hidden deep within
Until at last my eyes spied him

And whilst the mind fought hard and long
My heart just wasn't quite that strong

And as my soul gently woke
A heart I thought had all but broke

Slowly healed itself and then
My heart and soul became one again

This man with tender loving care
Healed a heart I thought not there

Until the whisper I first heard
Was loud enough to hear the word

And heart and soul soared high above
And the voice spoke the word and it was love

BECAUSE I COULD

You asked me why
I traded all my secrets to the dark side
You asked me why
I looked you squarely in the eye and lied

And even when you ask me why
I deceive and destroy and deny

I know that it's plain if I try to explain
My efforts will only end up in vain

For you will always be asking me why

FLAVOUR OF THE MONTH

A special smile
A glint in the eye
Don't stare in the sun
Or maybe you'll die
You thought you were special
I wonder why
Couldn't you tell
The truth from the lie
If the man had told you
That he could fly
Would you have stood
Staring high in the sky
Well, I've been to the sun
With a man who could fly
And I've stood on the ground
And stared at the sky
I've watched my life
Pass me by
For a special man
With a glint in the eye
And I'll never quite
Understand why
I ignored the truth
To live the lie

MATTER

This matter is no longer

Some people of course
Themselves for reasons
Not easily known
No longer matter

SOUL TO SOUL

Soul to soul
The width of outstretched wings
The spirit soars above the highest peak
I see the two souls entwined in strength
Breathing in harmony beneath beating hearts
Soft and silent, strong and spiritual
And higher than a voice could ever soar

LAVENDER BREEZE

Warm afternoon and the backyard breathes
Of a child with a cricket bat painted soft green

Little girls make flowers of wood
And woman paints as only she could

The lovers stand under sun so warm
Man circles them mowing the lawn

Tennis ball makes a whoosh through the air
As the men sit on logs sipping their beer

Plank of wood leans on upturned bath
Children slide and fall and laugh

Music fills the air with Ween
And the noisy child fills the space in between

THE GLOW

Passionate flame
Touching soul
Erotic devotion
Embracing whole

Warm familiar
Intense gaze
Secret spark
Informs blaze

Burning fingertips
Softly blow
Calm whisper
Forever glow

VIVID

You sprang from the density
Of a darkened desire
Alive
Aware
Intensely awake

And I opened pale eyes
To a new escape

Hoping my time had come
Knowing that I would leave
Anyway

The memory of your deepened colours
In my mind
Water on my lips
And a throat so dry

The halo above your head
Was so vivid

RHUBARB

Fearing the worst
He tiptoed in
On fingertips
Just in case
Her libido
Was sleeping

HOLD ON

Hold on to the hope
When all else has let you down
Hold on to the belief
That your time will come

Believe that with hope
You can overcome despair
Hold on to the faith
When nothing else is there

FAKING IT

I spoke the truth
Whilst fish around were faking it
I dreamt of swimming upstream
Never believing of making it
I stayed til I was sick
And tired of taking it
As if the dream had ended
And upon waking it
Seemed as if all the while
I'd been mistaking it
For the reality of a fishpond
Intent on faking it

GINGER

Courage (tangerine)
Mystical (berry)
Membrane (lime)
Explodes

Following close behind
Was irresistible energy
She thought it tasted like chocolate

Powerful and extroverted
Loudly thinking to oneself
Potent energy
(Potential)

SPECULATION

Once I stood alone on the edge of a cliff
And tried to free my soul
The day rolled clouds of grey
Silently over my face
And made promises that I could fly

My feet stood quietly amongst the rocks
Urging me to leap into the sky

I stood alone and listened to my head
Don't be a fool, it said
You'll end up dead

BLACK

Frighting my quicksteps
Leaving the nightling behind
Losing my mind

Biting my hindsight
Deep in the night
Losing my fright

FAVOURITE OF MINE

He was a favourite of mine
Clearly a momentary lapse in sanity
Held on with fear and loathing
And unavoidable craving
Until I opened
My tightly clenched fist
And let him slip seductively
From my fingertips

USELESS

Senseless longing
Sweeping gestures
Flattery will get you nowhere
Making it up as you go along
Longing senses and gestures swept away
Nothing to do but pray
Now what else would you have me say?

CHEATING AGAIN

Breaks my heart
To see you cry
Poor little boy
With the slut in your eye

Breaks my heart

VOICES IN MY HEAD

Why hello, how nice to hear your voice
What's that? You're doing well?
You say you have a new romance
Well, I think that's just... swell

Oh no, I don't mind in the least
I'm glad you're moving on
How could I think otherwise
For that's surely what I've done

Well, no, there's no one in my life

IF I WANT YOU

If I want you
I'll tell you how I feel
And maybe even kiss you again
I'll wait until you fall
In love with me
Then I'll tell you
If I want to

VOLCANO

The voluptuous kiss
Caught him by surprise
So much so that he mistook it
For a trick of the light

Surely such a twisted android
Could only imagine such bliss
Caught in the light
Of the voluptuous kiss

CLOUDWATCHING

I wasn't meant to live in this world
I was meant to live with my head
In the clouds
A dreamer never awake
I was meant to wish upon stars
And fly to the sun
And never feel feet touch the ground
I wasn't meant to live like this
I was only meant to live

EVERYONE

Everyone has the answer
Everyone knows the score
Whenever I think I'm getting it
Everyone's getting more

Everyone figures it out first
The reason and the rhyme
And whether or not I want to know
They'll tell me every time

SPARE THOUGHTS

The telephone rings incessantly
In my ear
Haven't even had my morning coffee yet
Sometimes I try to spare a thought
For others
But usually I haven't got the time

HEAVEN

I wish I were in heaven
No ties to these toes
Free to be an angel
Or however the story goes
I don't like money problems
Or children up my nose
I just wish that I were somewhere else
But where only heaven knows

RIGHT IN THE MIDDLE

He was having such a good time
When all of a sudden
He stopped

ALL I HAD

Possibly you wanted a stronger reaction
With news so shattering and savage
It seemed almost to me a kind of disappointment
In your eyes
Almost a cruel notion crossing your mind
But all I had in me was an
Oh

SEVERAL TIMES

Several times a day
I look at myself in the mirror
Is that pimple getting bigger
Is my hair a mess
Wonder what a woman
In one of those third world countries
Does with herself
Several times a day

ME THUNK

No matter if you're falling down drunk
Or falling down drunk
Or falling down drunk
(Too many bottles of red, me thunk)

Blessed are those
With the nose
Who knows
Maybe a red wine smells like a rose
Which by any other name I suppose

Would not make it sweeter to drink
(Me think)

So no matter if you no matter no more
I'll say no more on the matter (I swore)

For there's more to say on the matter at hand
Not meaning of course that you understand

Or even care
What I say (I swear)

But I'll try to be brief, direct, curt
Keeping in mind feelings get hurt

If you dig around a person's dirt
A person's bound to be brief, direct, curt
If digging around a person is hurt

Would it be awfully rude if I just turned and ran
(Frankly, my dear, I don't give a damn)
To how I might think (therefore I am)

But I really must say
Come what may
That I hope you have a happy birthday
Or a day of birth happy at play
Playing a happy kind of a day

For a birth of a hap
(A hapless chap)
Forced to read all this nonsensical crap

Or maybe it's just a non-fanciful crop
Whatever the measure I can't seem to stop

I'm doing the best that I can, my dear
But the reason for stopping is reasonably clear

If I don't stop now I'll run out of words
And, besides, this writing is for the birds

Alas the light is growing dim
Happy birthday, Kim

DREAM

When you are sleeping
And cannot hear me breathe
I shall place my kisses
Upon your dreaming lips
My soul will weave its essence
Into the soul of yours
And I will lie eternally
In the arms of the one I love

FADING

Sitting in a room
The sky swallowing the sun
Our features darken
As your face slips from my view
And I am left
Sitting in the dark
Alone

MORE

Wanting an impossible
I try not to ask
But it's all that I want

SOMETIMES I THINK

Sometimes I think people aren't listening
Because I have nothing to say
But sometimes, such as now
They listen anyway

HOT AFTERNOON

In the far-off distance
I can hear the sound of a dog
Barking

Sometime ago
A man walking by my gate
Made plans
To stop the noise

But I can hear the barking
In the far-off distance

Of course the man
Would have to walk
A long way
To reach the noise

I would think
He would have reached the dog
Round
About
Now

(Abruptly the barking has stopped)

PRETENDING

She was very good at pretending to cry
Pretending she was in love with the guy
She fooled them all but oh not I
I knew all along it was only a lie
She wasn't really pretending to cry

STOP THE RIDE
I WANT TO GET OFF

Stop the ride
I want to get off

PAIN AND SUFFERING

I used to think that suiciders
Were simply being selfish

How could they hurt
The ones they love

But I think, really, they are hurting too much
Themselves
To realise

And they died
Inside
Long before anyone noticed

A WEED

A weed stood in a magnificent garden
Surrounded by the most beautiful flowers
She had ever seen
Oh no, she thought
I do not belong here
It must have seemed to her
That any minute now
She would be found out
She sat amongst the flowers
Admiring their beauty
And feeling so much less
Than they
Until one day
A gardener discovered her there
And promptly pulled her out
He tossed her
On a pile of dried leaves
And she breathed a sigh of relief
For she knew all along
That she had not belonged

NO HOW

Let's not beat about the bush, she said
I wish I were dead, she said
And you do not
What a load of rot, he thought
I wish I were not here too, he thought
But I cannot express my thoughts
As well as she
Thought he

WHAT AM I SUPPOSED TO DO

When things inside
Threaten to engulf
My soul
And I don't know how
I'm ever going to break free
Tell me how
I can come back
From such an abyss
Of blackness
Losing sight
Of all I used to be

FORGOT TO BREATHE

I let myself shut down inside
And crept into my hole
No one saw me leave
Or even noticed me gone
I folded in upon myself
Let the waves of tears
Wash over the pain
Stubbed out the spark
That used to keep me going
Because I don't want it any more

FISH

Have you got a mediocre love affair
That can never reach
The heights of ecstasy
In one tremulous
Breath?

HIDDEN

She sits in a chair outdoors
And tilts her nose to the sky
She feels the wind weave breath upon her face
And opens up her eye

Leaves and branches loom above
Creating a life of lush
It wraps her up and hides her
Deep within the hush

And I can't see her any more

PIRANHA

Tastes like chicken

She needs to devour every inch of flesh
If she can't sink her teeth, tear and torture
She will eat her own skin

Tastes like chicken

She needs to consume
Every inch of his being
Strip all that remains
To satisfy her insatiable hunger
To bond and bind
And she loves

The taste of chicken

HE PAINTS

He paints upside down
Standing on his head
But the world is so twisted and turned
That no one notices
She studies his paintings on the wall
And wonders why they have all
Been hung upside down

NOSES

Noses run in my family, he said
And sometimes feet
Insanity runs in mine, she said
He frowned and thought aloud
That's not funny
I know, she said
Quietly inside her head

A DREAMLIKE STATE

I saw him standing over there
Looking so perfect
Everything I wanted
Standing so ready
I heard a noise from behind
And momentarily turned to see
And when I turned back
He was gone

WISH

A wish made twice
But both the same
One borne of faith
The other hope
Both looked at stars
And dreamt of love
And wished and wished
With all their might

TIDAL WAVE

Swimming against the tide
He found another strange creature
And together they swam to the blue

They were told that fish can't touch the sky
But together they flew

EATING FISH

She loves the way he plans his meals in advance
Whenever they eat out
He thinks a great big juicy steak
Is what he's hankering for
But he usually ends up eating fish
She just loves that

PASSION FISH

Hyperbolic
Snack
Interlude
Particle
Harmonic
Receptacle
Nitrogen
Broke

Table d'hôte

SNAFU

{Situation Normal All Fouled Up}

When the ocean is green
And the sky is pink
And things are exactly
As you think

When the purple fish
With the bulging eyes
Leaps from the water
And flies

Can you see
The sleeping squid
And do you know
What he did

I do

UN

Unabated unassailable unceasing unbar
Unwilling unkind unwelcome under

Uncover unclaimed undercurrent ungird
Ungrateful unbending unrefined unheard

Unrivalled ungainly uninitiated unless
Unlikely unofficial unspeakable undress

Unpopular unseasonable unworthy undone
Unbelievable unavailable undeniable un

COURAGE

He wants a love without the ache
She wants a heart that cannot break

They want to know that dreams come true
They do

THE DIFFERENT ONE

She stands on the back porch
And reads a story
Turning pages like a pro
Animated chat
Pictures facing out
For all to see

But she has no one to read to
But me

RAVAGE

Suspended warning
Flickering
In my mind's eye
Sensing unrest
In the middle beast
He can hardly
Stop himself
My mind is moving away
But he is not paying attention
To anything
Now

I SHOUT

I try to whisper but a scream comes out instead
Always screaming in my head

Wish I could whisper it out
But instead I shout

FORESIGHT

For you to see
What I can do
You have to know
You believe it too

DEAD INSIDE

I don't even have the energy to move
I know we should get out
And stay busy
Keep her mind occupied
At all times
But I'm too defeated
To move

OPEN WIDE

Jemima has a hat made out of paper
Simon colours green around the rim
Trisha has a doll made out of pretzels
And they both get up and sing

SKUNK

Skunk
Drunk on life
Skulks
Behind his wife
Drunk
Skunk on life
Behind
Skulks his wife
Skunk

LICKING THE LOLLIPOP

Juicy and sticky
Lips lazily lick
Tingles and tickles
Tongue touching tip

Tastes so terrific
Smacking my chops
Takes me to heaven
Eating my lollipop

POTATO CHIP

Tortured
With a chip
Force fed
All this bullshit

SHORT TEMPERED

The fuse is lit
Bottom lip bit
She has a habit
Of chewing off more
He understands
She secretly wishes
She were a man
She wants to lie down
In the dark
But she can't

SUMMER SHOWER

When I come out of the shower
And step into the dark shadows
I will feel warm and sensual
And you will cup my breasts
With your sensitive hands
And whisper that you love me
And my body will groan
I love you too

CUCUMBER KISSES

Cucumber kisses
Corn chips and crackers
Candles and chocolate
And cheese
(grated)

H E

He holds his breath
Lets out a sigh
Waits for her hands
To reappear
She can't keep them off
She wants to expand so much
To have and to hold
His breath lets out
A sigh

BLOATING

On a river in a boat
Sat a man with a bottle
Lots of thoughts in his mind
And an oar across his lap

Must have sat in that boat
On that river
All that day
With a bottle
And an oar
And lots of thoughts across his mind

Must be hard
With all that water

FATIGUE

Hollow sockets
Shadows sweep the moon
Leaden limbs balancing
On a memory
Tears
Without the energy
To cry

FURTHER AWAY

Just beyond my grasp
Fingertips skim the air
Remembering a time
They tangoed in your hair
It's nothing in particular
Just that you're not there

And I feel I'm floating
Further away…

BITCHING

Wrong hair colour
Wrong shoes, wrong shine
Wrong, wrong, wrong
Each and every time

Doesn't she know it
Hasn't she heard
What was she thinking
It's simply too absurd

What is she doing
And doing it for so long
Doesn't she realise
It's all wrong, wrong, wrong

MOURNING

He stands on the edge
Of a dark unknown
His toes curl carefully
Around rock
And moss

And I see his fear
And I feel his loss

He is wishing
That I were still in his heart

But he's forgotten
The colour of my eyes

ANGEL

She has the face of an angel
And the wit of the wicked
A smile so warm and sad

And you would not believe
The dreams that she's had

But perhaps that wonderful wicked wit
Is the cure

That will bring her back
From the brink

HIS BOAT

His boat
Capsized in the middle
Of the day
But it took
Him awhile to note

His head
Had been hanging
Over the side so long
He'd forgotten
He was still in the boat

SYNTHESIS

The curling of the petal-palm
Is only for a moment
A ray of light
Encourages the colour
Softly, slowly
The smoothness
Enraptures the touch
A firm beginning
Emerging from a shell

FINGERPRINT

To make an impression
You have but to press
In your case
You could do even less

LATE AGAIN

The strictness of the hour
Bled apprehension in her veins
Perhaps the singing siren
Had hypnotised his brain
And like a figment
She could recapture where she'd lain
And the uncertainty
Would surely get the blame

TRUTH

Some people whisper it
Some even shout it from the rooftops
Most only think it
But still the lying never stops

LOVELY VIEW

He lives in a cave
On a mountain
In the middle of nowhere
It only seems like he's here with you

Lovely view

CATERPILLAR CRAWLING

His belly
Lies close to the dirt
But with that armour-like shell
He rarely gets hurt
He crawls along inch by inch
I really think he likes all that dirt
Stupid me
I got hurt

CLOSED MIND

The mind's eye clicks into a corner of the room
She's still wearing pyjamas and it's almost noon

She opens the curtain and the darkness dissolves
Into her mind the eye revolves

Slowly
Blinking
Shut

ANGEL OF MINE

Angel of mine
With the demons inside
Hiding the truth
In the web of a lie
And I'd give anything
To see you smile
Deep within your heart

SO TALL

The smile was fractured
But in the stained light
It was easily overlooked
A fragment of glass
Jagged in the twilight
He probably wasn't smiling
At all

He slowly walked towards her
Not blinking
Not staring
And it wasn't until he was
Almost level with her mouth
That she realised his gaze
Was fixed somewhere
Over her left shoulder
It wasn't his fault
He was just so tall

EXCESS BAGGAGE

In the anything to declare department
She stood contemplating
Her predicament
To admit the excess
Would surely cost her dearly
But she'd already got away with lying
Well, nearly

If only her body language
Did not give the game away
But who the hell was she fooling
Anyway

MY IN-BETWEEN

You're not the one I want
You're not the one I need
You're simply the one who came along
To become my in-between

You think you're the bee's behind
My God, you must be blind

Haven't you guessed
You were second best
You weren't any different
From all the rest

In all other ways you were just the same
Except you stayed longer at the game

My forever in-between

VOLCANOES WHISPERING

Listening to the nightmare
Of volcanoes whispering
The violence echoes in my brain

How colourful the languages erupting
Between the emptiness of blame

CHAMELEON LIES

All this time I thought you were good
At blending in
Fitting in with me

Pretending this was where
You were meant to be

I mistook you for a part of me
For so long
That I didn't notice
You had never been here at all
It was only me

SUICIDE NOTE

This is the last breath
That I take
These are the last words
That I make

Wishing it were all over
Wishing I could close my eyes
The finality in my heart
Is the clue to my demise
Wishing it were all over
And I could close my eyes

Wishing these were the last words

VAE VICTIS

{woe to the vanquished}

On the tail of a zephyr
He pretended to fly
All the better to stay awhile

She laughed at his loss of dignity
(She'd pinched that long ago)
Ah well, how was she to know

She thought his true feelings
Had been hiding
Why didn't she know he was just biding

His time

KALEIDOSCOPIC

The overgrown eye peered intensely
At the ripened
(pause for effect) bud
A cucumbered sonnet
Wrapped in a tissue of
(pardon my French) crud

A feeling that some form
Of sin ee stir intention
Had gone (slightly) awry
The mind is capable
Of extraordinary invention
(thought the eye)

A picture of fermentable
(don't say it) bliss
And no plighted troth to betray the
(wait for it) kiss

The overgrown eye blinked
Once or twice
Just enough to shift it
No cause (for alarm)
The phantasm aspect
Only seemed like it was (twisted)

BARELY-THERE

A barely-there fleet of a thought
Fluttering foolishly to my feet
Sorrow mixed with I-don't-know
Stamping horribly hard
Must be my brain again
Dripping carelessly down the edges
Seeping into sanity
Weeping over the memory
Of an in-control life
Think I left it on the kitchen table
Yesterday

ROSEBUD

Striding purposefully into the room
His rosebud cheeks abloom

I'm out of breath, his puffing said
Running rivers through my head

He needs watching, the ladies cluck
Lets his feelings run amok

I didn't mind, I just stared at the moon
And dreamt of those rosebud cheeks abloom

WHEN I CLOSE MY EYES

When I close my eyes and think of your features
Running wild with the feral creatures
My skin tingles, my toes twirl
Even makes my eyelashes curl

Wouldn't change it for all the world
My man, my magic, my moon

I feed off the stars with a hunger so tight
Lisp of your lusciousness in darkest of night
Speak of the mystery in whispered tone
Of a force beyond anything we have known

Wantonly ache for passions unfurled
My man, my magic, my moon

Crystallised waters warmed by the sun
I know how deeply your rivers run
And I choose to ride the rapids unfeared
Craving the depths of creatures unreared

Slowly my secrets are being uncurled
My man, my magic, my moon

WHEN MY BIRTHDAY COMES

When my birthday comes
And I am older then
I will open up a new day
And begin my life again

GARBAGE

She pulls the wheelie bins up onto verandah
Rubs her dirty palms
And pushes wheelie bins around
She will spin them in a circle
Lift the lids
And let them drop

Push them
Pull them
Spin them
Sit them
And peer in from the top

Bump them off verandah
With an ooh upon the ground
She pulls the wheelie bins
Pushes wheelie bins
And circles them around

INTRICATE DETAILS

Intricate details
Weave accidently
Over knobbly bits
Passionate players
He bites
And he hits

And it's all okay
Coz he's been having a lousy day

Intricate weavings
Over delicate feelings

He bites
And he hits

SADNESS

I reach deep inside
Where my sadness lies
Feel the soft squidgy sides
Where my sadness cries
And it's hard to tell
Where the root of it lies
Deep inside
Where my sadness resides

LEAVING

He wants to leave but he can't go
He thinks of this she doesn't know

But his anger, frustration, and wrath she incurs
Until at last her memory blurs

She forgets the man who loved her so
And just sees the one who wants to go

SIMPLE LITTLE THINGS

It's the simple things you remember the most
A look, a smile, a touch
A careless word tossed away
That you barely noticed much

You didn't listen hard enough
You didn't see the signs
It's the simple things in life
That will get you every time

He said I love you a hundred times
So often that you forgot
And only seemed to listen
When he said he loved you not

He only said I don't just once
But that was all it took
A simple little thing
But not as simple as it looks

SMELL

I smell you on the bathroom towel
I'd smell your underwear but that's too foul

I smell your sweat on a hot summer's day
I roll in bed on the smell where you lay

I smell you in the air I breathe
The breath I take is the smell you leave

I choke on your smell, I suffocate and splutter
I even smell every breath you utter

I hold my breath, I block my nose
In the end I'll die from your smell I suppose

But I don't care if I go to hell
I eat, I breathe, I taste your smell

SEEMS A LONG WAY

I'm in a place I deeply revere
Where mind and soul are crystal clear
But I can't see you anywhere near
You seem such a long way away from here
If I squint you almost disappear
If I shout I doubt that you would hear
It's not a thing I greatly fear
But you seem a long way away, my dear

VEIN

Blood oozles from a broken foot
Glass cutting vein and muscle
Never mind about the hustle

Oozing bloody broken butchered dreams
I sit in vain and hear the screams

Didn't hurt I wouldn't think
Thought I saw the huntsman wink

He knows the truth about my pain
Bleeding broken bloody vein

SPIDERS

I opened my mouth
And a dozen little black spiders
Crawled rapidly out of my rotting skull
It's funny because I didn't realise
How long I'd been dead
I thought it happened recently
But where did all these spiders come from?
Maybe the mind was poisoned before death
Maybe spiders are in us all the time
I guess I learnt a lot
The day the spiders crawled out

THERE YOU GO

I wanted to eat out at a restaurant
See a movie on the big screen

Monday I cooked dinner
Tuesday was take-away Chinese
Which we re-heated on Wednesday
Thursday was pizza at a pub
And on Friday you were ill

No dinner at a restaurant
No movie on the big screen

Why do you always get sick
Whenever I want to get my way
And why is my freedom
Always wrapped up in your chains

And there you go
Doing it again

AND HE DRANK

I wonder why he was born at all
The lives he destroyed, the memories torn

A rotting evil who festered and stank
And he drank and he drank and he drank

A little boy and an innocence lost
A mother's fear and the price it cost

A childhood canvas beaten and blank
And he drank and he drank and he drank

Minds that don't know how to grow
A hidden side he never showed

All of this they have him to thank
And all because the monster drank

And he drank
And he drank

PITY

The creature's eyes were downcast
Staring intently at the black dirt
Scurrying black beetles
On a cold black day
A black hole
Gnawing away within
Pity
For at that moment
A magnificent
Colourful
Glorious
Creature
Flew majestically
Gracefully
Silently
Overhead

CIRCUS

A caravan rumbled into view
The circus had come to town

He stood on the sideline, excited and awed
With a secret desire to run away
And join the adventure

Suddenly a colourful acrobat
Leapt from the passing parade
And grabbed his hand

He was overwhelmed
By the spectacle and mystery
And felt afraid
But he did not stop her

She drew him into the drama
And showed him the life he had wished for

She seemed to draw her energy
From the noise and pageantry

She came alive on the trapeze
And with the thrill of it all

He couldn't believe
He was actually there
Amongst the greasepaint and sawdust

And that was the moment
When the circus magic disappeared
And he was left with the grease and sawdust

He ran away, back to his safe, quiet town
And breathed a sigh of relief

The caravan performers passed him by
And he thought he saw a tear
In the acrobat's eye

LOST

I was floating on a life raft
For such a very long time
I almost lost hope
Of ever being rescued

Sometimes a search plane would fly overhead
But they were too far away
To ever see me

One day a ship came into view
I didn't bother getting my hopes up
But the ship slowly moved closer
Until finally I could get excited

I didn't even notice my precarious grip
On an unsteady raft
Adrift an unmerciful sea

All I could see was the ship
Coming to rescue me

After a time the ship began to turn away
I watched it slowly get smaller
As it disappeared from view

And I sat all alone on my unsteady raft
Amidst the unrelenting ocean
And wondered if I shouldn't just give up
And let go

After all, my ship had already sailed
And the planes were too far away
To ever see me

WHISPER

A little whisper in my unlistening ear
Remember to look up at the stars
We can deny the outside
For as long as it takes
But the inside will always remain
And a kiss that can send
Its soul to the stars
Should never be squandered away

YOU

Midnight
Thinking of you
The more I know
The more I love
This is for you
There will be no other
You are the one
With the backward tilt
Edging closer to my endless horizon
I feel you from the inside out
I travel the globe
Dissect all insects
And you are the one I choose
Your outside is divine
Heaven on a stick
But your inside
Is better

INTIMACY

Whenever I let go completely
I become a stranger to myself
I am borrowing you
As if you no longer belong to me

FALL

I watched a leaf flutter
As if I had all the time in the world
Silly girl
Who has time for fluttering

PAPER THIN

A corner folded into triangle
A tear along the edge
And the suicidal woman
Watches a paper aeroplane
Glide weightlessly over the ledge

BREATHING

A slow-moving breeze
Like breathing or blowing
Tickles the back of her neck
Tiny hairs stand up on end
She knows the breathing belongs to him
She feels it
No matter how slight
It sends a shiver down her spine
A tingling, electric sensation
She knows the breathing
And it's only a little bother
Suspended in the back of her mind
The thing is, you see
She knows the breathing
But it isn't him
Because he isn't here
She is alone

SPILT MILK

No use crying
Over things you can't control
Your isolation and misery
Are all your own doing
Instead of your lonely existence
Waiting for your sometime man
To call at his own convenience
Why don't you find yourself
Someone who doesn't drink milk

OH NO!

It's raining again
Flattened hair and drips
Forming puddles at my feet
Shivering inside
Feeling bedraggled
As if all my emotions had drowned
And, yes, I feel like crying
But I can't
I watched the dark clouds forming
And now it's too late
It's raining again

KNOT

You tell me that you visit to keep me happy
You want to make it clear that you
Would prefer to stay away
And do I understand
I do
You would be happier
If you were somewhere where I'm not
And so in keeping me happy I am very clearly
Not

WOULDN'T IT

Wouldn't it be nice
To brush our fingertips
Between all that wishful thinking
I used to think I could bend steel
Now I wonder why I even tried
I wish I was the girl of your dreams
And that you were the man of mine
I wish I knew if that were true
But I tell myself so many lies
And my heart's too busy breaking
To give up all my secrets
I just know that I hear your voice
When I close my eyes
I see your face, I feel your touch
I remember your words
And the way you move
And I miss the shivery delicious moments
In my life

SECRET

Scratch the surface, pierce the skin
Let the secret seep right in

Beneath the skin, beneath the bone
You are mine, and mine alone

And despite its undisputed flaws
Know that my damaged heart is yours

RSVP

Thank you for the invitation
To your special celebration
Alas I cannot make the party
For I am not so hale and hearty
So after thinking long and hard
I write to you this little card
In the hope that though we're miles apart
My wishes reach your happy heart
All the best, my lovely dears
For a union that will last for years
And when you're old and slightly grey
(Though no one wishes for that day)
I hope your eyes still sparkle strong
With a love to last a lifetime long

FROM ONE EXTREME

You're not my friend
I've had my fill
You tried to destroy me
But I'm standing still

Your tongue is forked
You are a liar
And it feels like I
Have walked through fire

You tried to trample
On the words I speak
But your soul is black
And you are weak

I have no time
For friends like you
So full of hatred
Through and through

I know you live
Your life in denial
But take my word for it
You're vile

TO THE OTHER

I don't know why time moves so fast
I don't know what makes friendships last

But I knew the instant I met you
That I had found a friend so true

You opened your mouth and words spilled forth
And like a compass pointing north

I saw your spark light up the sky
And I can't really explain why

But I knew the moment I heard that sound
That my soul sister I had found

HERE'S THE THING

So here's the thing about poems that rhyme
It doesn't happen every time

Sometimes I'm blocked (like a rat in a drain)
Sometimes my thoughts are hard to explain

Sometimes I'm in a lousy mood
And can even be a little rude

Sometimes I'm busy with other things
Or when I'm creating, the telephone rings

Sometimes I'm not in the mood at all
(Hang on a sec, I'll just take that call)

Now where was I? Oh, yes, making excuses
For the absence of my creative juices

It's just that I know your demand is high
And I know that you want me to really try

But it's just that sometimes in desperation
I'm woefully lacking inspiration

And the poem that you eventually get
Just happens to be my worst one yet

So please do not let your anger vent
When you see the poem that I have sent

For intentions were good and I did try my best
But I fear that I have failed the test

And inadvertently dropped the ball
By giving you a poem about nothing at all

But worse than that, it seems that I took
All those bad poems and filled up this book!

Kerry Mitchell

Also Available

The Witch's Tale
{A book of rhyming fairy tales}

Coming Soon

The Bellwether Rules for the Dead
{A ghost story}

And

Theodora van Runkle
{Be careful what you wish for}

www.ingramcontent.com/pod-product-compliance
Lightning Source LLC
Chambersburg PA
CBHW030528010526
44110CB00048B/733